Liver & onions
Red wine & tears

Liver & onions
Red wine & tears

heartsongs for the non-conformist

Thisbe Lloyd

Copyright © Thisbe Lloyd, 2016

The right of Thisbe Lloyd to be identified as the author of this work has been asserted by her in accordance with the Copyright, Designs and Patent Act 1988

Printed by Lightning Source

All rights reserved. No part of this publication may be reproduced, distributed or transmitted in any form or by any means, electronic or mechanical, without the express written permission of the publisher.

Contents

Mother. Daughter	11
Warms hands; cold heart	13
Damned in the art	15
The boy at my side	17
The oak	19
Ramblings (i)	21
Ramblings (ii)	23
Daisy chains	25
Railway sailor	27
Door. Stop.	29
Waltzer ride	31
Heartsong	33
Tinderbox	37
Friend	39
Army of the hill	41
Totem	43
Broken	45
Dream makers	47
Ivy around my heart	51
Noise	53
The drowning	55
Hands	57
Insomniac's dream	59
First-Aid kit	61
Grand National	63
Wolf at the door	65
The cotton reel	67
Tempest	69
The physicist	71
Liver & Onions	73
Locksmith	75
Pompeii	77
End of the pier	79

To the one who believed I could fly.
Just like Fred Astaire.

Always.

"Atticus, he was real nice..."

"Most people are, Scout,
      when you finally see them."

– To Kill a Mockingbird

Mother. Daughter

From the corner of my eye,
Bright green memories.
You walk through my head
And leave your trace, as fresh as once was.

Her smile, is you.
I see in her eyes a glimpse of times, long since passed,
Where laughter sounds through forgotten woods
And falling stars of browns and gold
Lay, thick, on woodland paths.

Voices echo on the wind and toss through my hair,
Spinning memories I can almost touch.

From the corner of my eye,
You walk with me, daily.

Warms hands; cold heart

While we sit and talk, a lifetime goes by
In a whirling ball of greens and blues.
All the thoughts and the words of all of my friends
Spin, silently, round in my head.
For all will be gone on some rainy day.

When I hide from those who look for me.
As deep in myself I twist and I turn
Desperate to unravel the knot.
One twist too many and tighter it binds
Wanting so much to be free.

Explosion within and back to the start.
With face poised, teeth shining white
But scarred deep within which thickens again
And makes for a much smaller heart.

Damned in the art

My head is full of questions
My heart hides behind its door.
Strange tangles of disillusionment,
At my skin, they claw.

Hampered by my thinking,
Circling thoughts spin around within.
Whispering doubts and worries,
Shadows, now begin.

But, pale figures walk beside me,
Slipping in and out of sight.
Strength and faith they speak out loud,
Timid wings, take flight.

I hope they know I'm grateful,
Despite these faltering words.
Scared and fretful in my shape
But, voices always heard.

The boy at my side

Rings of blue hide a bright shining light
Switched on in an instance, but connection fails.
How to reach in and touch what is there?
Capture, embrace, ride with the wind.

The spark glimmers strong but dances out of reach.
A well timed quickstep, it flickers, dims.
Gone in an instant, relit only on its own terms.
Indignant, controlled, defiant, enigmatic.
To tame the storm that crashes the rocks
Eludes the most weathered of sailors.
But some will glimpse the clear waters below
Where mermaids live on, and things come to pass

That if you believe, with the strength of your soul,
Will take you by the heart and make sing!

"This is me!"

The oak

He stands taller than all around
With sturdy bark, war wounded,
Some reaching the innermost rings.
Yet his roots are strong and grip firm to the earth.

His branches shelter and protect,
Despite the fierce storms
That batter and strip bare his leaves.

His branches let through the light,
Softly kissing the ground
Allowing the warmth to bathe those beneath.

His branches reach far and wide,
Ever growing to accommodate those in need
Of a stable place to cling to.

He weathers the elements,
With a silent stillness.
Grounded and beautiful.
My mighty oak.

Ramblings (i)

So sick of fighting, falling short
Of expectation,
Standards,
Conversations.

Player picked for team B only.
Sub-bench.
On the sidelines.
In the trench.
Stop gap.
Time filler.
Question of convenience.

Ramblings (ii)

Glass globe, looking in.
Nose pressed as glitter falls.
Soft landings on figures held within.
But the border holds its shape.
Permission denied
To enter where snow drifts and settles on their faces.
Entry not permitted.

Access, not for you.

Daisy chains

Would you still marry me
If all that you see
Is the person who stands before you?

Would you still place that kiss
Or would our lips miss
If you knew what you know now?

Would you still fall in deep
If you got to keep
The whole package, in its entirety?

I'd fall time every time
With this heart of mine
And get lost with you forever.

Railway sailor

Striped, feet spiraling
Through a figure of eight,
You turn, ever moving.
Windmill arms.
They watch from afar
Unperturbed, yet aware.
Slinky shakes,
Twisted,
Bent out of shape
Yet, transfixing.
Just a touch to assure.
Time bends for you.
Stretched, as the plastic coils.
Shuffle steps.
Long jumper leaps.
Train arriving at platform 8A
Destination, Unknown.

Door. Stop.

My wedged angle, a sturdy grey
You wish to be enclosed, private?
Then pull me away.
Push me gently to the side.
I haven't vanished or deserted my post.

I stay, unused, until you need me.

You wish for a slice of air, but not too much?
My slight edge gives rise to opportunity.
Slide me in short
A slither of myself, for you.
The part may be small, but it is strong.

I stay, unused, until you need me.

You wish to hold the door open wide?
Then use my whole being.
Sit me close to the hinges, the base of the source.
No hands needed to hold or to steady
The breadth of my use is yours to choose.

I stay, unused, until you need me.

Waltzer ride

Spinning through, edges blurring
Dizziness of the unknown.
Gripping, knuckles white,
Fingers entwined and fixed to a movable bar,
In to corners unseen.

Fellow passengers, slamming together
Squeezing the very breath from my lungs.
Organs, bunched, confined, to breaking point.
A moment of relief, with others now the fulcrum,
Mere seconds of release.

The turn of events, never ending,
Speeding through the constant ride.
Stomach turning at a thousand miles an hour
At the mercy of the switch controller.
I want to get off.

Heartsong

The line has been drawn in invisible sand
But deep lays the line in its trench.
The gap opens wide and pulls with a force
That cannot be fought with fist clenched.
And anger and tears fill up in a heart,
A heart that saddens with age.
It weakens each day from the beatings it takes
And cowers in its prison and cage.

Its song softly sings, but quiet is it now
As the line marks the score deeper still.
For time has been marked with a much quicker step
Which cannot be followed at will.
So, lost is the heart and head follows too.
As they try and make sense of it all
When sky crashes down with all of its might,
No longer can head hear the heart's call.

Tinderbox

The ebb and flow of words
    dancing through the air between
Finding their way to the recipients' eager ear
Lighting up the space around, between, within

Deep, yet light in touch, tripping, leaping from lips
Poised, waiting to share, to connect
A song between the two,
    the lyrical charge igniting their breath

He sits, drinking her in,
    her childlike bounce in action
Her wide-eyed embracing of him, of them,
    of the ridiculous,
No subject taboo,
    scholar to clown with one stroke of her tongue.

The spark flies from the flint of their speech
Falling on the dry kindling of soul and heart.

Friend

The brightest star that shine in the sky
Sees not its aura from within.
But satellites encircling it, from dawn til dusk
Are entranced by its warm glow.
Some fly, not close enough
And retreat from the, sometimes, brilliant outer haze.

But those who have the courage and curiosity
To see what lies at the core,
Are rewarded by the softened waves
That emanate from its true centre.

When finally exposed,
The place that lies within is filled
With open fields of the most beautiful, fragrant flowers.
To breathe the air is to find calmness and fulfilment.

The light does not burn, but gently warms
And those the rays touch, are forever blessed.

Army of the hill

Twisted blades and emerald shields,
Rusting in the autumn blaze.

Fallen soldiers,
Cradled by a million mystics' orbs

Heart;
Strengthen on this high ground.

Heart;
Strengthen on this high ground.

The solitude of Dreamer and apprentice,
Buoyed by Sapphire skies.

Refreshed;
Static calmed, to the rush of a heart.

They travel on in their world,
Untouched by non-believers.

Totem

Landscapes shift,
Beneath her eyelids.
Warm suns beat down.
Soft tides whispering
Their love songs to the sands.

Mountains rise,
Deep Inside her heart
Rains soothe the fire.
Winds breathe change and hope
Yet never tame her wild.

Rivers course
Their waters run fast
Lost in the flow.

Serendipity.

Tranquility; in dreams.

Broken

Disjointed and lost, she sings to the crowd
The noise and the static rage far too loud.
Silence and order she covets and craves.
Humdrum and chaos, she'll take to the grave.

High up on the hill the wind whips through the spaces
When crashing down, sudden, she sees in their faces,
The mess and confusion, the distance between
What is now, what was then, and what could have been.

The ache, oh the ache, that hangs in the air.
The eyes cannot hide the yearning that's there
For quiet and those times when a smile fills a heart
How did it happen? Go back to the start.

Broken and shamed, exposed and bereft.
Mindscape all battered. There is nothing left.

Dream makers

Who says convention falls easy to all.
What linesman paints with such permanent stain,
That the borders are indelible?

Stood firm in their dream weaving; the immovable.
Sketching the lives of others,
In straight linear, drawn sharp,
As are their judgements.

Yet who appoints these creators of aspiration?
Who builds the materials list for their wares, dished out
To the clamouring masses.

What dreams are made of?
Stretched tight over canvases,
Shape shifting, like ghosts of reality,
    wandering through,
Out of my vision, at times.

Dancing wonders, holding shape, all but for moments.
Shifting, spinning, whirling, beckoning me on,
    to reach out,
Touching the indefinable substance.

Falling short of the expected, bent out of shape.
Stepping across arched planes,
Diverting from the applied
Parallels set in stone, by others.

Sit astride those boundaries. Set the criteria to you.
Myths and legends on the easels of others,
    are to their design.
Who's to say what dreams are made of?

Ivy around my heart

It is not governed by your haves,
Or measured by have-nots.
It simmers near the calm surface,
Inside it twists and rots.

Not guided by the moon or sun,
Nor money in the bank.
One day, you seem invincible,
The next hour simply blank.

No rhyme, nor reason, in its plan,
Or warning does it bring.
Cries of laughter once rang out,
Now, only noise and din.

So, judge me not on your beliefs,
Your eyes don't always see,
The crown of thorns around my heart
Jailing what is me.

Noise

Let me alone with my thoughts and holler and din
For to keep all these out, I just can't let you in.

His voice booms so loud, around in my head
All the pain and the anger from all that was said.

The venom and spite, the scorn and the lies
Still hold as fast.

Do you think of that now
Or
Do you blame me?

The drowning

Water levels rise,
Choking, clouding vision.
Flailing limbs,
Barely enough strength.
Limited air,
Lungs crushing inwards.
Mind imploding.
Static raging on high.
Darkness, alone,
Lost in an ocean of thoughts.
Vessel's sails;
Useless, tattered and torn.
Leaking hull,
Waves forever beating on.
Her eyelids closed.

Final sight

                    was

                                  your

                              lighthouse.

Hands

Folded, closed and tall.
Wrapped within, a space, between the towers.
An empty void? A measure of air?
A moment of thought, mind twirling rings,
Spun, in a musing moment.

Wide, bent with length and sagging knuckles.
A dance of movement, sweeping,
Embracing and receiving landscapes of others.

Marked with trenches, pathways.

Meanderers of time.
Time on your hands.
Tracing and mapping across the tight-knit material.

Hidden. Obscured.
Designed by others.
The blue bird's flight, feathers entwined with sinew.
Keeping safe the reminder
Of

Who

You

Are.

Insomniac's dream

Drawn up, pulled tight
She shrinks to the smallest she can be.
Back curled and bent
Don't touch.

Walled in, shut off
Kept prisoner in that lonely landscape
Arms crumpled and taut
Can't touch

Stiff neck, ratcheted arch
Chin joins thighs and knees up close
Noisy mind, misshapen
Won't touch

Delicate and damaged
She pulls herself back to that hidden place
Protected, yet jailed
Lost touch.

Delve in, reach out
Fingers knot around a rescuer's branch
Still, deep, out at sea
Please touch.

First-Aid kit

(*i*)
Encased in the safety of his arms.
Widening eyes waiting to take the leap.
Soft lips, planting Band Aids to a broken soul.
Taking the out of bounds route, because we can.

(*ii*)
Widening eyes waiting to take the leap.
Knotting fingers with the offered hand.
Taking the out of bounds route, because we can.
The tower builds from the strength of the core.

(*iii*)
Knotting fingers with the offered hand.
Entwined and locked in the open invitation.
The tower builds from the strength of the core.
Rising towards a moving sky, with stars, undiscovered.

(*iv*)
Entwined and locked in the open invitation.
Soft lips planting Band Aids to a broken soul.
Rising towards a moving sky, with stars, undiscovered.
Encased in the safety of his arms.

Grand National

Done with all the talk and noise
A single tear breaks open the dam
As the wave of hurt pushes through,
Charging black stallions surge.

Hollowed out, like pumpkin flesh
Leaving an unstable, delicate void.
A candle, lit, quickly burns down the wick
To a flicker, dimmed and faltering

She held it in her hand, momentarily.
It danced away from her grasp,
Taunting her with its double quickstep
Collapsed inward, she is flawed.

Wolf at the door

Oh to be a wolf, with air balloon lungs
To blow the darkening clouds
That build, stack upon stack,
Far away to distant shores
To release their downpours in to the sea,
Not down on me,
Just let me be.

Oh for a mighty pair of bellows, gathering air
To stoke the fire of hope
Whose embers falter and gasp,
dampened to a dull flicker,
Reignited to a roaring flame, rising through,
Up in to my heart.
Just let it start.

Oh to be an eagle, with wings of strength
To defy the downward pull
Of thoughts and monologues,
Playing out in a mind,
To soar away across mountain and tree,
Totally free,
Just let it be me

The cotton reel

Spread out ahead
A fine thread, unraveling, rolling.
Fingers, tips outstretched
Chasing its journey.

She stops, at times,
To look up; gaze to the horizon.
Eyes, wide, hungry,
Mapping its progress.

Bustling Cities appear.
Clamouring noise of life, happening.
Ears, funneling the mind fuel,
Imprinting memories.

Quiet seas, lapping shores.
Boats sail, to the point where water touches sky.
Skin, soaking in experiences
By osmosis; to savour.

Forests follow mountains,
Stillness of air, broken only by eagle's wings
Lungs, breathing in deep.
Life, love, being.

Tempest

Sat, curled, tight as a fern
Inward, to herself,
Minimising exposure to the elements,
Clinging to her very substance.

Wishing, waiting, hoping
for a warming climate,
But none such forthcoming in the dark.
Snailed fingers gripping to palms.

Heart song, pianissimo,
Whispered, inside.
Her voice squeezed and dampened,
With no one to hear or duet.

Skies open, awash with droplets,
Sinking through her skin.
Nourishing, rehydrating, new shoots.
She waits for the rain.

The physicist

Missing the sound from your lips
As words trip through the space
Between me and you,
And all other matter
That lays in the gap.

Missing the feel from your skin
With each silent touch, from tips of fingers
Between me and you.
And all other matter,
Removed from the gap.

Missing the beat of your heart
through the cage of my chest, mine follows suit
Between me and you.
And all other matter,
Dancing in tune.

Missing the song of your eyes
As lyrics speak through them,
Between me and you.
And all other matter,
Disappears.

Liver & Onions

The side street held them,
cushioned from the crowds.

Boats, drifting by, with their striped pilots
Pushing away from walls,
Each kick creating distance.

The evening sun shrinking,
Pouring its Kia Ora stains across her face.

Her green eyes glisten.
Memories flickering beneath
Forging their substance to the fore.

A lightness of heart
Trips across her soul in silent echoes.

This evening's menu choice;
Liver and onions
Red wine and tears

Locksmith

(*i*)
Unlocked by a key, cast with no mould
Mirrored eyes, circling, vocal, orbs.
The presence of a lilted smile.
To be discovered, seen, got.

(*ii*)
Mirrored eyes, circling, vocal, orbs.
Tumbling, spiraling in to the deepest well.
To be discovered, seen, got.
An unfolding of wings, feathers unfurled afresh.

(*iii*)
Tumbling, spiraling, in to the deepest well.
Warm black waters, drinking me in.
An unfolding of wings, feathers unfurled afresh.
Take flight, unburdened, safe, loved.

(*iv*)
Warm black waters, drinking me in.
The presence of a lilted smile.
Take flight, unburdened, safe, loved.
Unlocked by a key, cast with no mould.

Pompeii

When stripped away and bare
Heart ruins, all around.
The crowds are dispersed,
There is no more sound.

She now sleeps.

End of the pier

The shutters came down without warning
Closing him off
She looked for a way to gain access.
Shut down for the season

She retreated inside for shelter and warmth
She waited for him

And faded to grey.

www.ingramcontent.com/pod-product-compliance
Lightning Source LLC
Chambersburg PA
CBHW041219070526
44584CB00001B/20